CONCERNED
BUT NOT
CONSUMED
OVERCOMING
LIFE'S CHALLENGES

By Ron Sanders

© 2010 Ronald Sanders

Published by:
Zoe Life Publishing
P.O. Box 871066
Canton, MI 48187 USA
www.zoelifepub.com

All rights reserved. No part of this book may be reproduced or transmitted in any form or by any means including, but not limited to, electronic or mechanical, photocopying, recording, or by any information storage and retrieval system without written permission from the publisher, except for the inclusion of brief quotations in review.

All Scripture quotations, unless otherwise indicated, are taken from The New King James Version (NKJV) of the Bible copyright © 1982 by Thomas Nelson, Inc. The Bible text designated (RSV) is from the Revised Standard Version of The Bible, copyright © 1946, 1952, 1971 by the Division of Christian Education of the National Council of the Churches of Christ in the USA. The Bible text designated (TLB) is from The Living Bible copyright © 1971 by Tyndale House Publishers, Inc. Scripture quotations marked (NIV) are taken from the Holy Bible, New International Version ® copyright © 1973, 1978, 1984 by International Bible Society. Scripture quotations marked as (NLT) are taken from the New Living Translation Holy Bible. New Living Translation copyright © 1996 by Tyndale Charitable Trust. Scripture quotations marked as (NASB) are taken from the New American Standard Bible Copyright © 1960, 1962, 1963, 1968, 1971, 1972, 1973, 1975, 1977, 1995 by The Lockman Foundation.

Take note that the name satan and associated names are not capitalized. We choose not to give him any preeminence, even to the point of violating grammatical rules.

Author: Ronald Sanders
Editor: Zoe Life Editorial Team

First U.S. Edition 2010
Publisher's Cataloging-In-Publication Data

Sanders, Ronald.

Concerned but not Consumed; Overcoming Life's Challenges

Summary: In *Concerned but not Consumed*, Ron Sanders shares his victorious journey of rebuilding his life after a severe and devastating stroke.

13 Digit ISBN 978-1-934363-81-2

1   Detroit, Homicide Detective, Ronald Sanders, Stroke

Library of Congress Control Number: 2010925973

For current information about releases by Ronald Sanders or other releases from Zoe Life Publishing, visit our web site: http://www.zoelifepub.com

Printed in the United States of America

v2.1 11-22-10

Thanks /Acknowledgements

This book is dedicated to the following persons that encouraged and inspired me during the completion of this book. Names are too numerous to acknowledge, but I'll record just a few.

I would first like to thank my lovely wife Tina. Next, I would like to thank my father, Claude & mother, Bertha (deceased) and uncle, L. Dixon who is also deceased. I would also like to thank my entire family and specifically, my eight grandchildren; Lauron, Shayla, Mashanti, Markus, Jaquan, Lil' Ronnie, Christian and Cameron. As well as my cousins: A. Pegues-Miller, J. Stafford & M. (Mickey) Stafford-Brown. I want to give a special thank you to my caregiver for over 10 years, Mrs. F. Stevens and to my friends; Liz, John, Tony, Bobby, Moe & LaMont. I would like to thank my stroke doctor, Dr. K. Black and physical therapist, J. Muhammad. My previous pastors, Bishop David Ellis (deceased), Rev. Isaiah Patterson (deceased), Bishop G. E. Patterson (deceased), Rev. Dr. O. King III, Rev. J. Barlow (deceased), Min. L. Triplett, Min. V. Striggles, Rev. R. Baker, as well as my current pastor, Rev. Dr. W. R. J. In addition, I would also like to thank Deacon's, S. Pullum (family) and J. Douglas. As well as Judge Geraldine Bledsoe Ford (deceased). Lastly, I would like to thank my book editors: Mrs. D. Abston & Mrs. S. Lloyd, graphic designers: Mr. D. Greenway & Mrs. J. Nicholas and website designer, Mrs. H. Hayes.

CONCERNED
BUT NOT
CONSUMED

OVERCOMING
LIFE'S CHALLENGES

By Ron Sanders

Table of Contents

Introduction viii
Preface... x

Consumed
Wave of Good Fortune...2
The Stroke 4
Intensive Care Unit..6
Continued Hospital Stay..8
Quick Hospital Check Out..9
Rehabilitation/convalescence 11
Home Alone..13
Three Years of Self-Imposed Exile 14
Providence (Guidance of God) Drive 17
Firsts..19
Semi-Spiritual Quest..23
Miracles 25

Concerned
Short Commentary about Miracles 42
Serendipity or Godly Circumstances.......................43
The Beginning of a Real Spiritual Quest
(Nine Fruits of the Spirit) 45
Speech Problem/Public Speaking 47
God's Presence...49
Mission Possible 50
Speech Therapist 52
Another Part of the Master Plan 53
A Power Chair 54
Holier Than Thou vs. Real Inspiration....................55
Concerned Enough Not to Go to Hell 57
Ordinary People/Extraordinary People 60

God uses Ordinary People to do
Extraordinary Things 61

God's Blessings
Blessings 66
More Blessings 70
More, More, Blessings 73
Continued Blessings & a Role Model 74
An Almost Conclusion 76
Finally, Just Concerned but "Not" Consumed! 77
My Pastor's Favorite Benediction 79

About the Author 80

Introduction

I spent the majority of my career as a Detroit Police Homicide Detective Sergeant. While working homicide, I was involved in some of the most sensational homicide cases for more than nine years. One case involved the serial killing of eleven women. This case catapulted me to local notoriety and national fame. This notoriety led me to being photographed and featured in the popular magazine, "Vanity Fair." This new found fame also led to the signing of a Hollywood movie contract for the rights, to my police career. I even opted to have "Mr. Denzel Washington" play my part in the prospective movie. Just one month after my claim to fame, I suffered a severe and devastating stroke. I went from euphoria and utopia to severe depression and sadness.

I was led by God to do His will by sharing His work in my life for the benefit of others (primarily those with physical handicaps). However, this book is also intended to convey a message of hope to believers, nonbelievers and people without obvious physical handicaps as well. The central theme of this book is aimed at helping others cope with and not be consumed by everyday life problems. It is put forth as an instrument of encouragement and hope as you progress along the way to becoming more concerned with establishing a deeper, more personal relationship with God.

It was intended to be clearly written, so it can be easily and quickly read. This is my first book and I did not try to be the next Pulitzer Prize winner for journalism, or to write a literary masterpiece. I'm also not a Rhodes Scholar. My forte is police work and investigations, so this will be a plain, easy to understand, documentary of non-fictional events in my life.

Introduction

Furthermore, this book goes into great detail about how I became very depressed and angry with God for allowing the stroke to occur. I became consumed with the stroke and it's after effects. It also explains how several near-death experiences or Miracles occurred according to God's plan. I finally realized that the stroke handicap was a master-plan by God to truly have all things work together for the good, for those who love the Lord. And the master- plan over time made me see that my challenges and daily struggles matured me into a *"Concerned but not Consumed"* believer in Jesus Christ, my Lord and Savior.

One message that has stuck with me throughout my ordeal is that one must not be consumed by anything in or of the world but to be concerned about God and establishing a personal relationship with Him. One of my friends said, "After reading your manuscript I've realized that I've taken so much in life for granted. I need to get closer to God myself." This is my hope for you—it is the point of the entire book. Only a relationship with God can give us lasting peace, and I pray that this book will point you towards that peace. Finally, it was my intent to honor God and follow his instructions, by remaining vigilant and humble throughout the process of this book. I firmly believe in my heart, every person in this world has a story to tell! Thanks, ever so much, again!

Preface

Write the vision and make it plain, that he may run who reads it (Habakkuk 2:2 NKJV).

My memory takes me back a few years ago on a Saturday morning, and I've decided to put my thoughts and some of my past actions on paper. I prayed to God about what to write first. God led me to the scripture that says, *"In all your ways acknowledge Him; He will direct your paths"* (Proverbs, KJV 3:6). Therefore, I wrote this spiritually inspired book. With the thought that I would later reveal and write about my police exploits, some of which I've never shared before during the 23 years I served as a police officer in the City of Detroit.

A friend read the title of my book, *"Concerned but not Consumed"*, and said, "It's a very profound statement/title!" His following comment sets the tone for the entire book:

> *"The book title reveals that God wanted you to be concerned about your condition or challenge (stroke) and to do those things you needed to do. Taking additional physical therapy and eating the proper diet in order to get healthier, are examples. Instead, you were consumed about the stroke challenge. You were consumed to the point of hiding from family and friends.*
>
> *You were consumed in thoughts of how others would perceive you. You couldn't see or understand how everyone*

had genuine concern for you, despite the stroke. You didn't realize you were perceived by others as the same person post-stroke as pre-stroke. Furthermore, you are no longer consumed with thinking, "Why me Lord?", "But Lord, what would you have me to do?" "You want me to be concerned about getting healthier and to use the stroke challenge to help others?"

Another perspective or interpretation of this title could be that a person may say, "I want to be rich." Is this person saying they just want to have enough, to take care of basic needs for themselves and their family? This would equal concerned. On the other hand, another person makes the identical statement but is obsessed with hitting the lottery, excessive gambling, racetracks, or any other form of luck by chance. Then we can conclude this person is consumed.

Actually, this same comparison can be applicable to just about anything in life. It's my personal belief that satan tries to keep us consumed so that we are not concerned about God and what He has to offer. God offers forgiveness, prosperity, truth, and everlasting life.

In my (God's) book I attempt to illustrate throughout my personal journey, that I was so caught up or consumed with the challenges in my life, I *almost* forgot about thinking and being concerned about what was most important. What the Lord through the Holy Spirit offers is more important than anything on this earth.

1
Consumed

Wave Of Good Fortune

It was April of 1993; I was riding a wave of good fortune. I had just wrapped up a high-profile case of a serial killer responsible for the deaths of eleven women. I interrogated the suspect and obtained his confessions. I received several local awards and accolades from various civic organizations.

I also received national recognition. I had been featured, photographs and all, in the very elite and popular Vanity Fair Magazine. I signed a six figure contract with the Academy award-winning actor-turned-producer Timothy Hutton for the movie rights of my career as a Detroit police officer. The contract spelled out the arrangements for Mr. Hutton to produce a Hollywood movie of my 23 year police career. Wesley Snipes was reported to play the leading role. I had opted for Denzel Washington. Imagine that!

Something that everyone was overlooking, including me, was that the suspect had been captured by a hard working task force of local, county, state, and federal FBI law enforcement officers. All I did was obtain the confessions, but all the public and media attention was focused on Detective Sergeant Ron Sanders.

Admittedly, I was enjoying every bit of this attention; however, I was not giving God any of the credit or glory. I should have been giving God some if not all the credit for allowing me to receive this wave of good fortune.

At the time, I didn't realize that the whole ordeal—obtaining the killer's confessions and the subsequent media attention—was not a "me" circumstance. All the attention and accolades occurred in April. The stroke occurred one month later, in May. With that in mind, who do you think "didn't" get fame, credit or glory? I was literally devastated, after the stroke occurred! I felt all my hopes and dreams for notoriety were destroyed.

"THE" STROKE

My life as I once knew it both ended and began on May 22 of that same year. Does that statement sound contradictory and perplexing? Well, after suffering a devastating and debilitating stroke, I was left with a speech impediment and impaired balance. A strapping 6'1", 215lbs, Detroit Police Homicide Detective was left physically debilitated; dependent on a walker, and with many other minor health issues that manifested themselves as a result of the stroke's severity.

On May 21, I was vacationing in Cancun, Mexico. That night I suffered a very severe headache—the worst in my life. I, along with a friend from Detroit, walked to downtown Cancun. We spotted an ice cream parlor and ordered ice cream floats. I felt much better after drinking the float. The next morning was a Saturday, I flew back to Detroit and I felt fine. Once arriving in Detroit, I went to a birthday celebration for a good friend at a downtown hotel. I took one small sip of champagne and immediately became dizzy and fell to the floor. I was rushed to the city of Detroit's best emergency hospital. I can remember vividly asking the nurses to please hurry as they attended to me because I was on my way to a steak dinner at a famous Detroit downriver restaurant.

Unbeknownst to me at the time, I had suffered a massive stroke affecting both sides of my brain and a portion of my brain stem. I developed considerable swelling in my brain cavity. After several x-rays, it was determined I would be admitted to the hospital. Fortunately, my cousin was a registered nurse and supervisor at that hospital. She and my dad conferred with the doctors. They wanted to perform surgery on my brain. However, my dad and my cousin decided against it.

I was soon diagnosed with having suffered a severe blood bleeding stroke as opposed to a blood clotting stroke. In laymen's terms, a bleeding stroke occurs when a blood vessel bursts in your brain, causing bleeding into the brain. A blood clotting stroke happens when a blood vessel forms a clot or blockage of blood flow in a blood vessel in the brain. Both are serious and I could have died from either.

If I had died then, I most certainly would have gone straight to hell on a rocket! It's funny now, but boy am I glad God gave me a second chance! With what I know now and a description of hell, which I will share with you in a later chapter, I know for sure I was blessed and spared from eternal damnation, by God's amazing grace and mercy.

INTENSIVE CARE UNIT

After two or three days, I was transferred to the hospital's Intensive Care Unit (ICU). I was still unaware of how seriously the stroke affected me. At the time, I also had no serious thoughts about faith or God's mercy for that matter. That was a big mistake, as I learned later. Meanwhile, I was in ICU, hooked up to all kinds of machines, including a catheter. Trust me; being hooked up to a catheter is something you wouldn't wish on your worst enemy.

During this life-threatening experience, God was not at all in my thoughts. Even though I was a member of one of the largest churches in the city of Detroit, I was not practicing my faith. I was not giving praise to our Lord and Savior, like I should have, for sparing my life.

In all honesty and reality, I really had no clue about what it meant to have a personal relationship with God. I would soon learn that God, who loves us, knows how to get our attention. He may knock us off our high horse as He did Paul in the ninth chapter of Acts, or He may humiliate us because of our pride, as he did King Nebuchadnezzar in the fourth chapter of Daniel.

At that time, I was totally unaware that something non-physical was underway. My life took a drastic turn towards positioning me to produce all seven Fruits of the Spirit, recorded in Galatians 5:22. Now, I consider it more than mere coincidence that May 22nd, 5/22, and Galatians 5:22 brought fruition of purpose to my life. I have come to know that God does indeed work in mysterious ways. Also, that the Galatians passage led me to being concerned about eternal life (going to heaven), instead of being consumed by satan and "The" stroke challenge.

CONTINUED HOSPITAL STAY

When I came out of ICU, I began speech and cognitive therapy. I HATED IT! I hated who I had become. This was not me. This was not supposed to be happening to me! This therapy went on for another two weeks. Worse yet, the doctors and nurses couldn't understand why my blood pressure was staying so high and could not be stabilized.

Finally, my 1st cousin, the mother of my registered nurse cousin, who happened to be the supervisor on the floor, told her daughter why my blood pressure wouldn't stabilize. She said to her daughter, "It's no wonder that Ronnie's blood pressure won't go down. Your blood pressure wouldn't go down either if everyone visiting you were bringing you fried chicken, McDonald's, Wendy's, and Chinese food!"

When my cousin found that out, all of my little outside food and treats were cut off. I was BUSTED! It was for the best though, because shortly after that, my blood pressure stabilized and I was transferred to a rehabilitation hospital.

QUICK HOSPITAL CHECK OUT

I stayed there one—no, only a half of—a day. I was assigned a hospital room, and all was fine until this male nurse came in and said, "I'm going to be your nurse and I will be taking "gooooood" care of you." For some reason I didn't like the way the nurse said that. The tone was unsettling to say the least, especially since I was completely disabled and helpless against any questionable "gooooood" care. I immediately called my youngest son to come and get me; I checked out of the hospital against doctor's orders.

I suffered for leaving the hospital early due to my ignorance. The nurse probably didn't mean anything by what was said. As the term goes, IT IS WHAT IT IS! I learned years later my son caught a lot of flack, from family members for assisting me in checking out of the hospital early. But, what was a sixteen year old son to do? He didn't want to disobey his father.

As it turned out, I made an unwise decision. My premature checking out of the hospital because of what a nurse said, was just plain ol' dumb on my part. I had to be rushed to another nearby hospital, later that night, due to minor complications. I was not admitted to the hospital but I had to wait hours in the emergency room.

It was while there that an important revelation occurred (but I didn't take heed until years later). "I" wasn't, Mr. Important, Mr. Famous Police Homicide

Detective, Movie-making, Accolade-receiving, Magazine-featured personality. I was just an ordinary average "Joe Blow," sitting in a hospital hall on a gurney waiting my turn like everyone else. God saw to it then, and to this day, that I was completely humbled.

REHABILITATION/CONVALESCENCE

My next memory was of being in a rehabilitation nursing facility. The little faith I did have at the time and the tender mercy of God's grace got me through this 6-8 week convalescence ordeal. I was still in denial about my condition, and I was very negative towards the reality of this stroke. I literally had become hostile. This hostility was displayed to family members, friends, and convalescent facility staff. It was evident, particularly to facility staff. I was taking physical, speech, and cognitive therapy. I would start the therapy daily, from 8:00AM to 4:00PM. It was like going to a job.

I faced simple tasks such as re-learning to tie my shoes, walking, talking, swallowing, and going up and down stairs. The most humiliating experience was the beginning of speech therapy. I remember having to sound out C-A-T and other simple words.

I rebelled by not going to scheduled therapy classes and becoming really obnoxious. I was unprepared to deal with the reality of being victimized by the stroke. Just two or three months prior I had been riding the high clouds of good fortune. Now, having to sound out words like I was in kindergarten was the ultimate humiliation and required genuine humbleness. Really, I was only hurting myself with this type of behavior. Instead of acting as Moses did in Exodus 4 and not allowing my speech impairment to set limitations for me, I chose to be consumed.

The realization of this stroke permanently leaving me handicapped still had not set into my psyche. Nor, did it occur to me that this stroke would leave me permanently living a different lifestyle.

I also remember seeing my grandson, my oldest son's child for the first time, at about 5 or 6 month's old. I thought to myself, "This child is more advanced than me, a 44 year old man in the prime of his life." At least my grandson could crawl.

It was there at the convalescent facility that my bishop from my large church visited me and told me to "Look up." It took me twelve years to realize what he really meant.

HOME ALONE

Once, I finally left the convalescent facility I went home to live alone, with some help from my youngest son. Again, God was showing me grace and mercy and I didn't even know it. Prior to the stroke, I lived alone for several years but not handicapped and in a wheelchair.

Before the stroke I was very happy and comfortable with living alone as a bachelor. I was married for twelve years and, afterwards I lived alone in an apartment for three years. Then I lived common-law, for approximately six to seven years.

For those who know me personally they might be surprised to discover that I loved living alone. With my outgoing and gregarious personality, it did not appear to them that I was, and always have been, a loner. Although, I enjoyed living alone I am now happily sharing my life with my new wife.

THREE YEARS OF SELF-IMPOSED EXILE

While I convalesced at home, I shut everyone out from seeing me except some family members and my barber. As I look back on it, I think it was pride and embarrassment. I couldn't hold food utensils properly. I couldn't swallow normally. Even though I didn't suffer any disfigurement or paralysis (which, itself is a blessing), I was still self-conscious of my situation. In fact, realization of the stroke and its after-effects were finally beginning to set in. I was deeply depressed.

I literally kept my window blinds closed the entire three years. I read later that light helps to heal depression, and that modern medicine attests that there is great value in bringing a depressed person into a brightly lit room. (Nelson Holy Spirit Bible, pg. 765)

There are a few facts that stand out in my mind during those three years. First, my mom cooked my dinner faithfully every day. My father brought the dinners like clock work, day after day. This became a daily bittersweet moment. It was the highlight of my day for my father to bring the dinners, but he would always linger. Under normal circumstances this would have been just lovely, but because of my condition, I just wanted to be left alone.

He would stay and constantly stand over my shoulder, while I ate. He was always saying, "Ronnie,

Ronnie, Ronnie, hold that cornbread in your left hand, that's good therapy." To be quite honest, I didn't want any thought or type of therapy, especially during the only highlight of my day. Remember, the partial title of this book is consumed? My father and I now tease each other about it.

Second, periodically one of my best friend's would come over. This is amazing because several years prior, this friend was shot while working on the Detroit Police Department. I didn't know him at the time, except by name. I went to visit him while he was in the hospital. Unknown to me at the time, he would approximately 21 years later become a real worldly savior, in my time of need. Examples of this sainthood include: taking me to a favorite uncle's funeral wake, my youngest son's wedding, and a host of other places and occasions post-stroke.

Third, there was this Emmy-award winning, homicide TV show entitled "Homicide: Life on the Street" that I watched every Friday night. The reason this show was so significant was due to the main character. It seemed as though he interrogated murder suspects identical to the way I did. This character's personality was very, very similar to mine. What really got my attention was during one episode, this same character suffered a stroke on the TV show. As I identified with this character, I began to wonder about things we call coincidences in life.

Fourth, my barber friend gave me a shave and a haircut, every two weeks; come rain or shine for an entire three years. This was definitely a part of God's master plan for my life, because my barber is also an elder in a church, and he became a life-long friend of mine. Later, I will reveal how significant this barber friend became. I will say, he never once brow-beat me with religious talk. He never demanded that I attend church or pray; the whole three years he just faithfully groomed me. Little did I know he was ministering to me by his character, demeanor and actions! He groomed my heart, as well as my head.

The fifth and last, significant event during the three years of exile is very humorous. One day my youngest son visited me. He showed me how his laptop computer operated. I was amazed and giddy. I thought, "Wow, I can communicate with the outside world and no one will know I have a speech impediment, oops I mean problem."

Now, here's the funny part. My son and I had this standing joke that went like this.... IF SOMETHING AIN'T RIGHT, THEN SOMETHING'S GOT TO BE WRONG (referring to my three years of depression). This joke and my observation of the laptop computer sparked a fuse of change. This allowance of change is what moved me from my inner city flat in Detroit to a spacious apartment in the suburbs.

PROVIDENCE (Guidance of God) DRIVE

The move to my suburban apartment on Providence Drive marked the beginning of another chapter in my life. After I moved, I opened my window blinds wide, everyday, even though I still preferred to be anti-social. I also immediately purchased a desktop computer.

Believe me, even until this day I'm not a computer whiz. I still type "hunt & peck" style. I mostly use my computer for typing letters, looking up things through search engines (so I can be a brainiac), and sending and receiving emails.

When I first purchased the computer, I did visit a few chat rooms. A funny incident occurred one night. I had been visiting this one particular chat room. I kept observing this one individual, with a real provocative screen name. He (I guess/assume it was a male) would always enter the room and intimidate everyone. So one night, while this individual was in the chat room, doing his usual intimidating, I typed in, "Hey, buddy I'm tired of your stuff, you've got issues, and I'll beat you down!" The intimidator immediately left the chat room, very meekly and without a whimper. I guess he had never been challenged. Little did he know I was a handicapped, ex macho homicide detective.

Remember now I was still "The Man" and had that police detective demeanor, even in my situation. I believe this incident became one of my defining moments. I say this, because in the past I was too passive, meek, humble, and embarrassed to exert any type of real authority in my every day life.

My girlfriend started calling me the generic, "Hon." This had never been done in the past. I was "The Man;" I was "all that and a bag of chips" or so I thought.

FIRSTS

There were several "firsts" that occurred during my three or four years at this apartment (Providence Dr). Although many significant events happened, I'll expound on just three, one humorous event and two semi-serious.

First, whoever said, "It only takes one man to change things," was correct. I would write numerous complaint letters to CEO's of different companies, about situations or people who'd ticked me off. I always got results. I found out if you want something constructive done, you should just write a professional letter to the company CEO. Letters were sent to my Internet provider, major chain stores, my security company, apartment landlords, senators, congressmen and women, and all types of other organizations.

I really became good at writing letters and getting results. I also wrote a few letters for family members and friends. This all came to a screeching halt, one Father's Day. I went to this restaurant, with one of my sons and his then fianceé. I ran into one of my brothers and his girlfriend. By the way, two of my three brothers and I were all members of the Detroit Police department. All three of us were/are well known throughout the City of Detroit and its police department.

Back to my Father's Day story. I kept talking about some complaint letter I had written. My brother said,

"Hey, look, nobody wants to hear about your problems, everybody has their own problems." I became secretly angry but I thought about it and I found that I had become excessive with my letter writing. I later learned, from self-evaluating this issue that I was acting out through my excessive letter writing, the frustrations of having this stroke.

I know I said, three instances but I had to slip this in, especially to the nonbelievers. **God is real!** I once kneeled down to pray and I said this, "Please, God do what you do." I take God seriously and everybody should. However, I'm sure God has a sense of humor. Otherwise he couldn't be closer than a/my brother.

A man who has friends must himself be friendly,
But there is a friend who sticks closer than a
brother (Proverbs 18:24, NKJV).

Get it? Then the second semi-serious issue came, I finally started to use the telephone. It seemed that every time I called a business or whatever, I could not be understood or they thought I was drunk. This became very frustrating. Every phone call, I would start the conversation with the following introduction: "Hello, my name is Ron Sanders and I have a speech impediment, can you understand me?" Almost every time the person on the other end would reply "Uh, Uh, Uh, no, I don't understand you. Are you drunk?"

I reached my maximum frustration point one day. I called a business and gave my standard introduction, "Hello, I'm Ron Sanders. I have a speech impediment can you understand me?" The person on other end said, "Sorry, I don't understand you, what kind of disease did you say you had?" It's funny now, but back then it was just another demeaning, humiliating insult I had to endure because of the stroke. This is why I often refer to my speech disability as a problem instead of an impediment. An impediment can be referred to as a disorder or hindrance (something that prevents you from excelling). A problem however, is difficulty that has a proposed solution. Although, sounding different from others is difficult, my solution is being committed to improving and moving forward. I refer you again to Exodus 4, specifically verse 10:

Then Moses said to the LORD, "O my Lord, I am not eloquent, neither before nor since You have spoken to Your servant; but I am slow of speech and slow of tongue" (Exodus 4:10, NKJV).

Moses is one of the most significant characters in the Bible; he conferred with Pharaoh, the powerful ruler, to lead the Israelites out of Egypt. Yet, as this verse explicitly depicts, Moses had slow speech—a verbal handicap.

Third, and I still laugh about this now and it happened several years ago. I use to order a carry-out dinner from a restaurant every week. This day my carry-out dinner order was wrong. I called back to the restaurant. When an employee answered the phone, I said, "Is your manager AVAILABLE?" The employee responded, "My manager is not INVISIBLE!" Needless to say, I started laughing so hard I just kept the wrong dinner order and hung up the phone. "The" stroke at least did not deprive me of a sense of humor.

The next phase of my life, after moving twice, began my spiritual quest. I was well aware, by now, that the stroke and its after-effects meant permanent disability. If you've noticed all throughout this book I've always referred to my medical condition as "The" stroke not "My" stroke. That's because I've never claimed "The" stroke as mine.

SEMI-SPIRITUAL QUEST

It's now eleven years subsequent of the stroke. I was living in an apartment penthouse, with cathedral ceilings and a large living room sky window. I only mention this description because I didn't enjoy it. Even though the penthouse was very nice, and even though God was blessing me, I was blind to it all. I was too consumed and still semi-negative about the stroke. The stroke had occurred all of eleven years ago.

Again, several significant events in my life took place during the next three years. First, I joined another church. This was my son and daughter-in-law's church. I attended faithfully, every Sunday without fail. (My semi-spiritual quest, huh?) I would tell church members God was really blessing me, but in reality, I didn't know it. I would attend church even if the snow was deep. Certain members would comment, "I wonder why so and so didn't come to church, they don't have a handicap challenge like you." I would just smile and keep walking. If they had only known, how I felt inside, at the mere mention of the word HANDICAPPED.

Apparently, by not attending church post-stroke for eleven years, I held this mistaken belief that somehow God had mistreated me by allowing the stroke. I later learned "The" stroke turned out to be really a blessing in disguise (I was on a rocket to hell, remember?).

As I said, I had not attended a church regularly in the eleven years, after the stroke. I internally came up with all kinds of excuses for not attending church. It's a good thing I wasn't called home then (died). I surely would have been on that rocket.

MIRACLES

MIRACLE #1

I will share this incident, along with several other near-death incidents (Miracles) I experienced throughout my life. Then I'll return to the chronological order of events. I came to the conclusion that I MUST share these experiences, so you'll know the depths of God being real; His wonderful mercy, His amazing grace and my personal spiritual quest to the present.

I was getting dressed in preparation for a dinner engagement with my cousin (the registered nurse) and her husband. I had taken a shower and dressed, when I loss my balance and fell—striking my head very, very hard against a plastered wall in my bedroom. I put a major, humongous dent in the wall yet; I got up as though nothing had happened. I went to dinner and did not experience any pain whatsoever. I never mentioned this incident to my nurse cousin, until years later.

The next day I went to hospital emergency just as a precaution. I took x-rays but there were no ill effects, none. I thought it was simply amazing, Miracle #1. Just wait until I begin telling you of all the several near-death experiences, or Miracles, I can remember occurring throughout my life.

I hope they will give you clarification, of God's mercy and grace. In addition, demonstrate my need to share this book. I want nonbelievers to know the unequivocal awesome miracle and real power of God!

To be clear, these instances are not incidents where somebody told me second hand; but first hand accounts of incidents (near-death experiences, Miracles) that actually occurred in my life. Some of these incidents I've never shared with anyone. You will be the first to know. Again, I must expound, I'm only sharing these experiences (Miracles) to make the point: **GOD IS REAL!**

MIRACLE #2

Although Miracle #1 was used first to explain a point, it actually occurred much later. This is where it all begins!

When I was 2 or 3 years old, my family and I visited my maternal grandparents in St. Louis, Missouri. My grandfather and grandmother lived in an upstairs flat. There were numerous very steep stairs leading up to the upstairs flat.

This is what I was told, because I was too young to remember. I somehow managed to walk to the edge of the top of the stairs. My grandfather's dog, Trueboy came and stood in front of me, preventing severe injury or certain death. If I'd fallen down those stairs it would have been all over for me at the age of 2 or 3. Would you believe I don't like pet dogs today, ironic, huh?

MIRACLE #3

The next several near-death experiences, or miracles happened, during my 23 year career as a Detroit police officer.

In the past, there were a lot of snipers that hated the PO—lice. I was the driver of the scout car one day, when I proceeded to turn the vehicle around by pulling into an alley so I could park in front of this particular restaurant.

In the split-second that it took me to drive forward to turn around, a shot rung out, shattering the car window directly behind me. Surely, the sniper was aiming at my left temple. I believe the instant in which I drove towards the alley to turn around, saved my life.

MIRACLE #4

I was at the scene of a barricaded armed woman. She shot a rifle out of her living room window. I heard the bullet whiz very closely by my left ear, as I was crouched down behind a police scout car. If I had made a move one inch in any direction, I would not be speaking about this miracle.

MIRACLE #5

My partner and I were in police uniform, along with two uniformed suburban police officers. We went to an apartment building, to arrest a subject for a "robbery while armed" warrant. I knocked on the apartment door.

The suspect asked, "Who is it?" I responded, "It's Billy, man."

The suspect opened his apartment door and pointed a 45 caliber pistol directly at me, about 12 inches from my face. I tried to melt backwards in the hall wall. The suspect realized immediately we were the police, so he closed the door without firing the weapon. We rushed into the apartment and arrested the suspect and confiscated the gun which was in a skillet of hot fish grease.

MIRACLE #6

I was working an undercover assignment in plainclothes, in what was called an all precincts, city wide, four-man police crew. We supported the precinct two-man scout car crews. This was several years back before I became a detective. We were driving down a main street on the east side of Detroit, when we observed a man with a gun run into a bar. Thinking the armed man was going in the bar to rob it, I, along with my three partners entered the bar all in plainclothes. The armed man and I stood face to face, about five feet apart, both pointing our guns directly at each other, in what is called a classical Mexican Standoff.

My partners were standing directly behind me yelling at the man with the gun, "Police, Police, drop the gun!" Through the grace of God the man did not shoot me and dropped his gun. We learned that the man with the gun was the owner of the bar. He had chased someone out of the bar, just as we had observed him entering the bar.

I also learned from the owner, that he was going to shoot me because I didn't have time to produce my badge and he thought my three partners and I were hold-up men, due to our plainclothes.

MIRACLE #7

I was still working this plainclothes assignment some days later, only this time, as a two-man crew on the west side of Detroit. My partner and I were patrolling, when we observed two men standing on a corner. One of the two men was wanted on an outstanding warrant for "robbery while armed." I exited the driver's side door, heading in the direction of the wanted suspect, when my partner must have observed something I didn't because he started firing several shots at the suspect. There was only one small problem…I was in my partner's line of fire and several bullets whizzed by my head, just narrowly missing me!

MIRACLE #8

Again, several years ago I was working a two-man precinct car. While on patrol, a dispatcher call: "Robbery, armed, just happened," was broadcasted, along with the perpetrator's description. My partner and I proceeded to the vicinity of where the robbery occurred. I was working the passenger side of the police scout car (called the jumper). As we patrolled the area we observed a male about 18 years old exiting an alley. He fit the description of the robbery suspect. The suspect was observed in the immediate vicinity of where the initial robbery occurred. I exited the scout car alone and attempted to interrogate and frisk search him for weapons. As I was doing this, the suspect continuously kept trying to pull something from his rear pocket. The suspect and I struggled. The suspect continued to try to pull an object from his rear pocket. My partner remained in the scout car (the entire time) while I struggled with the suspect.

Fortunately, another two-man scout car was across the street from where I, alone continued to struggle. The other scout car crew assisted me in finally subduing the suspect. I retrieved a homemade zip gun from the suspect's rear pocket (a zip gun is usually described as a crude improvised single shot pistol/firearm). The gun I retrieved from the suspect was made from Popsicle sticks and a rubber band. The zip gun was loaded with one 22 caliber bullet. Had the suspect been able to pull the zip gun in such close proximity to me, I most certainly could have received a fatal wound.

Two notes, regarding the incident I just described. First, did you notice the emphasis placed on the word alone? The reason for this is the irony of my scout car partner receiving an award same as I, for capturing the suspect.

Second, this past Christmas one of the officers that assisted me in apprehending and subduing the robbery suspect visited me from Las Vegas, where he now resides. Even though the described incident occurred over 30 years ago, he remembered it in detail, especially, the part where my scout car partner never exited the scout car, until after the suspect was arrested and subdued. There are often situations where we seem to be all alone, but the Lord is most certainly with us.

MIRACLE #9

One year, I was working a special assignment in conjunction with the Michigan State Attorney General's office. This assignment was called Special Detail 318. Why it was called Special Detail 318, I have no idea to this day. However, the assignment consisted of approximately twenty police officers, whose assignment was to bring to justice crooked police officers working at a particular Detroit police precinct. A part of my assignment/function was to guard potential witnesses who would testify against the police officers.

One summer day I worked the afternoon shift, 6:00pm-6:00am. I arrived at a secluded motel room, where some of the witnesses were being guarded. During this shift change, another officer assigned to the detail picked up his personally-owned department approved sawed-off shotgun. When the officer picked up the shotgun, it went off. I was standing approximately 4 feet away from the officer and shotgun, with my back turned. When the shotgun went off several pellets struck me in the back. I yelled, "I've been shot!" I fell to the floor but no blood appeared. It turned out I was just sprayed with some pellets (much like the highly publicized shotgun incident, involving Vice-President Dick Cheney). I never even had to go to a hospital.

MIRACLE #10

On this occasion, I was off-duty and in my sergeant's police uniform. I stopped at this familiar party store, located on a main street, in the city of Detroit. I was behind the counter and bullet-proof glass, talking to an employee. A man entered the party store, grabbed a case of beer, and then ran out the store. I exited the store in an attempt to ascertain what direction the perpetrator escaped, in order to give the information to the responding officers. When I exited the store and looked north, the thief immediately started firing a weapon at me, while hiding in the alley in the rear of the store. I fell to the ground and returned fire nine times from my 9mm Smith & Wesson automatic pistol. I might add, I shot and emptied my pistol of nine bullets, nine times, in record speed. Again, it's funny now but not at the time.

After I ran out of bullets, I ran back in the store behind the bullet-proof glass. I urgently asked if there was another gun on the premises. But the employee said no. I was not shot or injured and the on-duty police arrived and captured the shooter. He had traveled some distance away but was arrested and placed in custody. He was also not shot or injured; Bad aim on my part. I joke with my son that in situations like this you don't really have to aim, just throw some bullets toward a perpetrator and they will usually get the message.

I later learned that the stealing of the case of beer was just a ruse to lure the store employee out of the store to kill him. I also learned that the shooter and the employee had a prior verbal altercation. I know one thing for sure. Even though this incident took place some time ago, I can take you to this party store now and you will still observe one of the perpetrator's bullet indentations that ricocheted off the building's outside east wall.

What's so scary is this bullet indentation is chest high, in direct line with my left chest area. Had the bullet gone straight and not ricocheted off the wall, it would have surely gone into my chest and to my heart.

An interesting note is that after that incident, the party store employee became a Detroit Police officer. I spoke to him recently for the first time in at least 15 years. He told me, "Thanks for saving my life because the person I argued with at the party store meant to kill me."

MIRACLE #11

Many years had past and I was working as a one-man precinct, uniformed patrol supervisor. I responded as a backup to a two-man scout car crew. It was during a pre-Halloween day. I believe the police run was "Family trouble or Family disturbance." The three of us arrived at the residence at the same time. I took a position by standing to the left of the door, and the other two officers stood on the right.

We are trained in the police academy to NEVER stand directly in front of any door you're about to enter, even during non-threatening police runs. You never know what's lurking behind a closed door.

The front door opened, one of the police officers on the right pushed me so hard that I almost fell backwards. He saw that the man that opened door had an 8 inch butcher knife concealed behind his leg.

After the man was placed under arrest, he told us why he came to the door with the knife. The man stated that for some reason his mind told him to stab the first man who entered his house. By all indications that would've been me. If I had not been pushed by the officer I would have been the first to step in. The man further stated that he was going to stab with an upward motion rather than a parallel or horizontal motion (side to side). What this means is, if the man had carried out his deed, I surely would have sustained a serious if not fatal stab wound to my stomach or chest.

I later worked at the Homicide Section with the officer that pushed me out of the way. He'll never know the magnitude of my gratitude for that push, because we never discussed it, but as you can see I'll never forget!

MIRACLE #12

I was working patrol supervision at a west side Detroit police precinct when a desk sergeant took an anonymous call. The caller reported that on a particular corner within the precinct (area of jurisdiction), two men were seated in a vehicle with a gun in the glove compartment. The caller further stated that the two men were there to kill a Sergeant Sanders because he harassed and arrested too many drug dealers on this particular corner in the precinct.

I immediately got up to respond to this anonymous call, but was ordered by my shift lieutenant not to go. Instead, a two-man scout car was dispatched to the location. Approximately, ten minutes later the scout crew arrested the two men and recovered a gun in the glove compartment.

When the two men were brought into the precinct station, I instantly started a conversation with them. They more or less confirmed, boastfully, "Yes, we were there to kill you." One of the men went so far as to say, (I quote verbatim) "Yeah, I know where yo momma and daddy live." Folks, I was not saved at that time so I won't repeat what I said or did!

MIRACLE #13

This miracle was the saving of the life of another person. I believe it shows that sometimes God uses a person to be a vessel to carry out a miracle for someone else.

I was having lunch with a Detroit Police executive officer at a restaurant within walking distance from police headquarters, in an area called Greek Town.

While eating, an elderly female at an adjacent table started violently choking. I immediately went to the woman's aid, and I learned she was choking on a piece of bread crust. I began performing the Heimlich maneuver. After several thrusts, the bread crust was dislodged from her windpipe, saving her life.

The woman wrote to both me and my police chief to express her gratitude, and she said she was the widow of a retired Detroit Police officer. It was extremely satisfying and meaningful to have saved a life, but knowing it was the life of a retired officer's widow uplifted me to an even higher level. God, God, God!

MIRACLE #14

There was also a time before I became a detective when I worked as a uniformed one-man patrol supervisor. I use to patrol a main intersection on the west side of Detroit. Drugs were sold rampantly on the corners of this intersection.

On this particular day, I was patrolling the corner on foot. As I walked across the street, a regular dope addict that I observed daily spoke under his breath as we passed each other. He said something on the order of, "Hey Sarge, you better hurry up and go to homicide because they're going to kill you."

I was amazed that this drug addict warned me that I'd be killed. I was even more amazed and perplexed at the fact that I didn't even know my transfer had been approved to go to homicide!

Nevertheless, not even a week later, I was transferred to the Homicide Section. To this day I wonder how that street drug addict could have possibly known that I had put in for a transfer to the Homicide section (and that it had been approved).

MIRACLE # 15 "THE" STROKE

Finally, it was the near-death experience, (Miracle), on May 22nd. Remember that date (5-22)? It was the day I suffered the devastating stroke. My doctor referred to me then and to this day, as her Miracle patient. She explained to me that in all her 30 years of practicing medicine she has never had a patient, that suffered a stroke as severe as mine left with very few post stroke effects or paralysis.

MIRACLE # 16

As I returned from my mailbox one day, I was reminded of one more near-death experience (Miracle) that occurred. Inside my mailbox was a short note left by my postal carrier. The note was about sharing her vacation cruise to Mexico. I had vacationed in Cancun, Mexico earlier than the time mentioned previously. Cancun is and has been my personal Shangri-La (Eden) world destination.

On this earlier vacation to Cancun, I went on a snorkeling tour (first time I ever snorkeled) in Cozumel, Mexico. Cozumel is a short distance from Cancun. The tour had come to an end and approximately thirty people had returned to the boat. The boat was cruising away. I was still in the water, gasping for my breath and watching the boat leave. A sudden fear gripped me because I thought I was going to drown.

You know that old saying, that when you're about to die your whole life flashes across your mind? I was so scared NOTHING flashed across my mind, except that I was about to drown. Fortunately for me, two Mexican young men, part of the excursion, dived from the rear of the boat and saved my life! I would have kissed them but I thought about that earlier experience with the male nurse!

It's humorous now, but it wasn't at the time. What's really strange is the fact I'm writing about each of these events from memory as though they happened yesterday.

Simply, amazing again! I'm amazed at these incredible incidents like I experienced them for the very first time. It's as if I'm writing from various outer body experiences. This is the reason for my constant astonishment. Don't even try to tell me there's no such thing as Miracles or God's master plan for your life. I've just cited 15 or 16 near-death experiences, Miracles, which have occurred throughout the years of my life.

"HALLELUIAH, HALLELUJAH, HALLELUJAH!" Why all the praise you ask? Well it's now one glorious evening fourteen years after the stroke and I walked over fifty (50) feet, unassisted by either walker or cane. The walk was unsteady; however, I was able to maintain my balance, without falling the entire fifty feet (50) or more. This is very significant for two reasons. First, one of my previous concerns was walking without a walker or cane. I can feel God's absolute power (don't you?). Second, a few months prior to that, my pastor sent out a taped telephone message stating, "I'm praying for all my church members to receive a Miracle." For sure, this counts as another Miracle, along with the others I've already mentioned!

2
Concerned

SHORT COMMENTARY ABOUT MIRACLES

Short commentary, regarding *MIRACLES*: (Taken from the January 1st, 2007 *Daily Word* magazine, by Rev. Tom Thorpe). The word miracle comes from the Latin verb that means "to look at."

When we look at the most ordinary things, events, and people with the intention of finding God in them, we are sure to experience miracles...lots of them. The great scientist, Albert Einstein once said, "You can choose to live life as though everything is a miracle, or as though nothing is." Whether or not you see the miracles happening in your life is up to you. Many of life miracles will not be seen, and not everyone's life story includes an *Obvious Miracle,* but you can always find a miracle...if you look for it.

Me, I have been blessed with many *Obvious Miracles;* my life's story, from A to Z, has been a miracle.

What's so strange is that this commentary was in the Human Interest Section of the magazine, which I never read. I think I may have read two in over twenty years. Was it divine intervention or another *Obvious Miracle (blessing)* which led me to read this commentary on miracles?

SERENDIPITY, OR GODLY CIRCUMSTANCES?

In the same issue of the *Daily Word* magazine, I read another story about a *Miracle*. It was titled, "Surrender into the Miracle," by Kathleen Lowndes. I was drawn to it.

Ms. Lowndes had brainstem surgery in 2003, and experienced almost identical circumstances as I did with the stroke. I've got goose bumps, just reliving this story. Our dilemmas were so similar in circumstance that when I wrote to her, spelling out the similarities, I joked "I hope you don't think I'm plagiarizing your *"Surrender into the Miracle"* article!"

I used my old detective skills and phoned Ms. Lowndes, at her home. She was elated that I contacted her. We shared experiences and the medical part was similar in just about every stage; recovery, ICU, life changing, feeling helpless, relearning basic minor tasks, experiencing a miracle, etc...

There were just two distinct differences in our experiences. First, she had brainstem surgery, which I figured was more extensive and quite severe, especially the aftermath. Ms. Lowndes explained that, *"The"* stroke I had was more severe. I think she was just trying to make me feel good, because you *know* anytime a doctor has to cut any part of your body, it's serious. I had to agree with her that it didn't make any difference rather

her injury or mine was the most severe. What mattered most of all was that we were miraculously still here; both living alone, with little help and no major disfigurement or paralysis. In addition, she's also writing a book to tell the world what God did in her life.

The second difference is she had faith and recognition of God during her entire brainstem surgery experience and ordeal. I didn't start recognizing God's goodness in my life until much later. In a nutshell she was positive throughout and I was negative, until I came to my senses. She said something that stuck with me, "Today is a better day than yesterday. Tomorrow will be a better day than today." What a quote!

The good news is that we're both still alive to tell you about it and to help those in similar circumstances. I've found Jesus and now we both live to praise him. We know that there's no 2nd chance once you die!

After reflecting on the *Miracles* that I have encountered, I feel the need to continue on with the true meaning and purpose of this book.

THE BEGINNING OF A REAL SPIRITUAL QUEST (NINE FRUITS OF THE SPIRIT)

First, the nine *Fruits of the Spirit*, (Galatians 5:22, NKJV) are Love, Peace, Joy, Longsuffering (patience), Kindness, Goodness, Faithfulness, Gentleness, & Self Control. So far, I've only acquired eight of the nine Fruits post-stroke. I'm still working on longsuffering (patience). Eight out of nine isn't bad. However, you all pray for me! I just heard a sermon and the preacher said his biggest nightmare would be him standing before God and saying he didn't do his best. I personally think God would definitely not be happy with me if I went up in there talking about, "Well God, I got eight of 'em (Fruits) right, but I just couldn't get all nine" (I think that rocket would be fueling up).

Anyway, in August of 2004 my spiritual quest really, really began. I went to my barber/elder's barbershop. After I received my haircut and shave, my barber asked me to listen to this radio taped message. It was a recording of a sermon, but the minister had a speech impediment (problem) that was worse than mine. I thanked my barber friend for the head's up and left.

I had no intention of listening to any recording. Remember back when my father was telling me to hold the corn bread in my left hand because it was good therapy? I had a disdain for people constantly telling me or referring that something would be good therapy for me. So the rest of that month, August and half of September went by. I hadn't listened to the preacher with a speech impediment, oops, I mean speech problem.

I knew I would have to get my September haircut and shave. Therefore, I reluctantly went on the Internet to listen to this radio message because I knew my friend, the barber, was going to ask me about it.

As they say, *"The rest is history!"* I listened to this tape of a Preacher Man, who had Cerebral Palsy since birth. His speech problem was more incoherent than mine. Yet, he had been preaching the gospel for over 30 years, to over 100,000 people annually. I was simply amazed and awe-struck! I was instantly inspired, after listening to that "preacher man." I thanked my barber ever so much, for directing me to that recording.

He was the same friend that gave me a haircut and shave every two weeks for three years, during my early post-stroke days. Remember how he never brow beat me about religion or church-going? If he had, I probably wouldn't be writing this book.

I guess God agrees timing, and more timing, is everything. Was my barber/friend directing me to that message as part of God's plan for my life? I know the answer.

SPEECH PROBLEM/PUBLIC SPEAKING

From the Preacher Man's inspiration, I volunteered to give a public speaking presentation at an upcoming Men's Day program at my church. This program was held on November 14th, at the church I previously joined earlier that year. Prior to this date, I had been so embarrassed about my speech problem but here it was, 11 years after "The" stroke, and I am *volunteering* to speak publicly in front of 200 people.

As the date drew near and with the encouragement of the pastor, I found myself really looking forward to speaking. Public speaking is supposed to be the number one fear of individuals, but God took away all my fears and reservations. Even so, I still had two problems. First, when I spoke, saliva built up in my throat. To rectify that, I asked my former speech therapist to assist me. She showed me how to breathe properly which eliminated the saliva buildup.

Second, I had a bladder problem. I feared that I would be in the pulpit and would have to leave, on my walker, to use the rest room, which was way back in the rear of the church. Before the event, I prayed about it. I gave my presentation and listened to the entire program. It was not until four hours later, at a restaurant that I even thought of using a rest room. Prayer does work!

Everyone said I did well. My biggest satisfaction came in two forms. First, a church sister came up to me afterwards and told me she had just had major surgery. She said that post-surgery, she had been a little down, but after listening to me, she was really inspired.

Later, an assistant pastor of the church told me he had a slight speech lisp that prevented him from preaching his trial sermon. To tell the truth, I never detected a lisp. That assistant pastor preached his trial sermon approximately two Sunday's later because, he said, I inspired him!

GOD'S PRESENCE

That same evening, I said my prayers thanking God for all He had done. I lay down to sleep and the strangest feeling I've ever had in my life came over me. The best way to describe this feeling is that it was like a warm glow saturated my entire body. Yet, I had goose bumps going down both my arms. I concluded that it had to be God's presence!

Anyone who knew me from pre-stroke days knew I wasn't even close to being a real serious religious type person. This is why I know this experience was significant and real. I believe at that exact moment and the steps leading up to that moment was not only life-changing but started me to look back over my life. I also believe it was preparation for things to come.

MISSION POSSIBLE

You've all heard of *Mission Impossible*, the old TV show and the Tom Cruise movies. Well, I want you all to understand why this book and my *MISSION POSSIBLE* are so important.

What I mean by this is simply...My mission for living, my sole life purpose, is to spread *the Light of Jesus and the Good News that God is real.* I've been volunteering to speak to stroke survivors at hospitals, and while there, manage to slip in the good news about Jesus. Since these are secular audiences with diverse faiths, I am careful not to offend anyone. Once I begin speaking specifically in churches, "slipping in" the good news will be obsolete.

In November a few years later, I submitted a written daily meditation, entitled "Mission Possible", to the biblical magazine *Upper Room*. I submitted the daily meditation with the hopes that millions of handicapped and physically-challenged people around the world would read it. I wanted to let them know that the mission, to spread the good news about what Jesus our Lord and Savior has to offer, is possible. Secondly, I wanted to inspire handicapped and physically-challenged persons to know that they don't have to be *consumed* with their challenges but can, and must, take part in this Mission Possible.

To those of you who do not understand, or who are not believers ponder this quote from *The Purpose*

Driven Life by Rick Warren: "if you will commit to your "mission" in life, no matter what it costs, you will experience the blessings of God in ways that few people ever experience. There is almost nothing God won't do for the man or woman who is committed to serving the kingdom of God." This powerful passage is what led to me to write this book. That is how much it inspired and affected me.

You'll get tired of me counting blessings later. I've received many blessings before I even made the decision to commit my life to serving God for His kingdom. It's like God already knew what I was going to do. Now, that really was a *DUH* (dumb) statement on my part (God knows all).

SPEECH THERAPIST

I spoke publicly again a year later, at Eastern Michigan University. This time it was for a Speech Pathology class taught by my speech therapist, the very same one who helped me prepare for my first public speaking event. Yes, in addition to being a speech therapist she is also a college professor.

My speech therapist was still assisting me, eleven years after the stroke. I met her during my three years of self-imposed exile and she genuinely gave me speech therapy that helped my speech problem. I found out years later that she was also a good friend of my cousin, the registered nurse, and that they are members of the same church. Am I alone, or can you see how this Miracle is a part of the master plan, created by God for my life.

I am completely amazed and flabbergasted at how God has orchestrated my entire life. It is almost unbelievable!

ANOTHER PART OF THE MASTER PLAN

Something else occurred that I feel is a part of the master plan. I have always watched the news at 6:00 p.m., everyday for over thirty years. On this particular day all the news channels were bombarding viewers with a news item that I was not interested in, so I switched to a local cable channel. Lo and behold, I saw my stroke doctor on the screen instructing viewers on a new stroke physical therapy procedure. This is the same doctor who said I was her miracle patient.

I had not seen this doctor in about 11 years, and I had mentioned her at stroke survivor presentations, but never by name. For the first time, I mentioned the doctor by name in my first big public speaking presentation, just a few months before I saw her on TV.

As a result of seeing my stroke doctor on TV and later speaking to her about it, I resumed physical therapy at the hospital where she worked. I tried the new physical therapy procedure that she spoke about on TV. As a result, I was able to walk short distances with a four-prong cane instead of a walker. This shows God's master plan unfolding because the new therapy changed my ability to walk. If I had not seen her on TV, I may have not found out about the new procedure.

A POWER CHAIR

After I completed the therapy, I thought I might want a power chair. I applied to a national company, but they immediately refused to cover the power chair under my insurance. I just kind of forgot about it because it was not a necessity but a luxury—even though I did want to beat my granddaughters in a race to the park behind my apartment.

After a couple of months I received a phone call stating, "Mr. Sanders your insurance company has just approved the cost of your power chair; we'll be bringing it in a couple of days." That's when I found out that unbeknownst to me, my family had secretly decided to all chip in to buy me a power chair. Had the insurance company not come through, I still would've had a power chair through my family's generosity. I hope you all see this "double" blessing from God.

I "knooow" you all are thinking I must be taking liberty with the truth. Do you think for one minute, I would jeopardize getting my heavenly wings and going to heaven after all I've been through? I think you all know the answer to that!

HOLIER THAN THOU VS. REAL INSPIRATION

During this time, I read the very popular *Purpose Driven Life* by Rick Warren at least four times cover to cover. That book, along with the recorded message by the Preacher Man with the speech problem, were two of the most inspirational things in my entire life.

Notice, I didn't mention the near-death experiences, *Miracles?* I was too dumb to know that God had a master plan and a purpose for my life. And, I didn't realize they were all the amazing grace of God.

It took a devastating stroke for me to take the time to actually think about and to realize certain things. Now, I can tell people I'm doing better now post-stroke than pre-stroke. As my pastor said, *"Never put a period where God places a comma."* How true this is! My early post-stroke attitude was *consumed;* I thought my life was over, period. God thought differently, and He punctuated that point of my life with a comma instead. I'm no longer consumed, I am now simply *concerned.* I hope you folks reading this book are inspired to turn towards God now, and don't wait, like I did, for something drastic to occur to make you change your way of thinking.

We all know certain individuals, that as soon as something drastic happens or they face a challenge in their life they suddenly get *holier than thou religious.*

Sometimes this individual is not really sincere but is simply trying to make amends for the drastic occurrence or challenge they're facing so they can hurry up and get through it. Often times this spontaneous religion doesn't last long. The spontaneity of this religious fervor only lasts until the challenge heals or ends. Then this individual goes right back to their sinful ways.

I want you to know that this is not the case with me. I am truly inspired. My Religious Belief is for real! I've studied long and hard about the true complexity of God. I have listed specific instances where I know beyond any shadow of doubt that **God is real!** "The" stroke was a definite wake-up call. It got me to thinking about God and what life really is all about. In addition to preventing my death—physically and spiritually—God has truly inspired me. These reasons alone are worthy of genuine praise and worship to God.

CONCERNED ENOUGH NOT TO GO TO HELL

I'll share with you why it was a blessing, as I describe hell. In all of my years I have never read or heard a depiction of hell, as chilling and descriptive as this. It literally, scared me and changed my mind, in terms of believing in eternal life after death.

Question: What is hell like? (Luke 16:23, NKJV)

Jesus said "hell was a place of worms, maggots, fire, and trouble" Jesus also said that "hell would be *outer darkness, weeping and gnashing of teeth.*" (Matthew 8:12, NKJV). Here the image is one of terrible loneliness: separation from God and man. Those who are consigned to hell will be put out into the inky blackness of eternity, with nobody to turn to or talk to—constantly alone. They will suffer the remorse of knowing they had the opportunity to come to Heaven with God but turned it down. There will be no exit, no way out from hell, **no second chance!** That is why it is so important in **this life** to receive the pardon that God extends to all men and women through the Cross of Jesus Christ." In other words, *"repent before it's too late and be saved"* (Revelations 20:11-15, NKJV).

I know many of you are familiar with the Scared Straight Programs. After reading and thinking about the hell description, it kind of puts your mind towards those programs. There is only one big difference; a person gets a second chance to do right in the programs.

Note: I've learned a lot of people in earlier years were SCARED into being SAVED. My description of hell, contained within the pages of this book by no means represents that one should be saved out of fear. I talked to a current older minister to gain insight in this area. He said, "the church of today doesn't expound on (a person) going to hell as much now because the concern is to preach that people live a wholesome life here on earth." He further stated, "if a person lives a life by what is contained in God's Word (the bible) they can be saved that way." The consequences of not living a God feared life or ever being saved, results in one going to hell, but it's not said just assumed. In other words, in most of today's churches the emphasis is placed on the now living versus the hereafter consequences.

While you're pondering the hell description, think about the following quote;

"I would rather live my life as if there is a God, and die to find there isn't a God, than live my life as if there isn't a God and die to find out there is a God." — Unknown

I almost forgot, I recently gave a public speaking presentation to about fifty youth, at an incarcerated youth facility. I don't know if it was me talking about that hell description or the incarcerated youth minister preaching, but over twenty of the fifty youth turned their life over to Christ during altar call. A demonstration of God's power! Again, simply amazing! "LOOK OUT, MR. PREACHER MAN!"

ORDINARY PEOPLE/EXTRAORDINARY PEOPLE

Consider the following daily meditation by Prabodh Diarsa: *"What could be extraordinary in our ordinary lives? The love of Jesus Christ that enfolds us is extraordinary. Our experience of being born again in Christ is extraordinary. The countless blessings that Christ showers upon us make our lives extraordinary. Christ's care for our daily needs and our anxieties is extraordinary. Christ's grace and guidance, which lead us to achieve difficult goals, make life extraordinary and serving God in certain situations is an extra ordinary privilege."*

Now you can fully understand how all of us Ordinary folks can be considered *Extraordinary*. As my cousin told me when I was preparing my first speech problem presentation, *"God uses Ordinary people to do Extraordinary things!"* Any ordinary person can be used to spread the good news of JESUS to the world.

Let everything that has breath praise the LORD. Praise the LORD! (Psalm 150:6, NKJV)

GOD USES ORDINARY PEOPLE TO DO EXTRAORDINARY THINGS

I am an example of how an ordinary person can make a difference. I used to be a common everyday police officer. I'm now handicapped with a speech problem, but because of that problem I'm using the same talent I used to obtain confessions from murderers to convert **nonbelievers** to believers, to the glory of God. I would say that's extraordinary!

Note: I use speech problem quite a lot throughout this book. No, I don't have a complex about my speech problem. I just thought it was important to keep driving the point across that despite the speech challenge or any handicap, a person can and should continue to press on.

The Bible says; *"that we should rejoice if just one sinner is converted (repents) and goes to heaven"* (Luke 15:7 & 10, NKJV). I would love for someone (an ordinary person, such as myself) to come up to me and say, "Hey Ron, I read your book and I have truly turned my life around." That conversation alone would make writing this book a success. Specifically nonbelievers, you've tried everything else, why not try God?

Speaking of nonbelievers, this following quote by an unknown author sums it up best; "I would rather lose at a cause that will someday win, rather than win at a cause that will someday lose." In other words, readers of this book may not necessarily turn their lives around now, but later on in their life they may remember a seed was planted by reading this book. Thus, perhaps winning in their life and going to heaven.

I've also adopted this very appropriate quote by Oprah Winfrey; "The key to realizing a dream is to focus not on success but the significance and then even the small steps and little victories along your path will take on greater meaning." For example, if the dream is going to heaven, a person can focus on *concerning* themselves to live *unconsumed* one step at a time, while here on earth until they get to heaven.

3
God's Blessings

BLESSINGS

Before I end this book I want to share with you several of my blessings from God. I've received many since I actually began to realize they were blessings, in other words since the night of November 14th. The list is quite extensive so please bear with me. I won't cite them all. I'm only citing them to show readers of this book, how a person can be rewarded by just following God instead of the world. Please, think and ponder on that! I feel I must share them with you. That way you'll be able to recognize and count your individual blessings, despite how insignificant you think they may be.

First, I joined another dynamic church (my second, post-stroke and that I won't name, due to my past profession). I joined after visiting the church on my uncle's invitation and first checking it out. I needed a church home closer to my residence. What has most impressed me about the church, is the pastor. She requires all church members to bring their Bibles to church every Sunday. Every Sunday, it's a sight to see when my pastor asks the entire congregation to lift their Bibles in the air, just prior to the sermon. In addition, my pastor is a teaching pastor. This enables me to understand the biblical word much better.

Second, I became a church mentor for teenage boys as well as an eleven year old boy. This was a blessing because after, 23 years on the police department, I was accustomed to dealing with teenage youth, after they got in trouble. Being able to help youth, especially males, before they get in some trouble has been very rewarding for me, and is a true blessing. Also, I have been blessed to be the church senior high school student advisor, helping seniors obtain college scholarships.

Oh, there's one other interesting God master plan phenomenon, as it relates to my current church. Something happened years ago, while I was at the rehabilitation nursing facility. Think back to when the Bishop of the large church I belonged to visited me (I'll never forget what he said because he's deceased now)? The Bishop stood by my room window and pointed at the sky and said, "Look up, look up." I never fully understood what the Bishop meant until much later after joining my current church.

After I joined my present church, God's master plan for my life was still unfolding. I learned Psalms 121 (NKJV), is one of my pastor's favorite scriptures. The first verse says, *"I will lift up my eyes to the hills from whence comes my help..."* Is this not amazing or what?

My favorite Bible verse for years has been Psalms 37:4 (NKJV), *"Delight yourself in the Lord and He will give you the desires of your heart."* As I continue to cite my different blessings, you will see why the aforementioned Bible verse is my favorite and is starting to become true and real.

Third, although I was once diagnosed with borderline diabetes I no longer take medication. After losing about 40 pounds, I control the diabetes with only diet and exercise. This is something that I have also overcome, throughout my life's challenge with "The" Stroke.

Fourth, a friend of mine told me "It would be a sin for me not to share the knowledge and experience I have about police work." I thought this statement was kind of strange, coming from him since he has always been my mentor in police work. His faith in my abilities was a blessing. It reminds me of one of my favorite quotes which says, *"You are the sum total of your life experiences"* (unknown, author), how appropriate.

Fifth, my barber/elder friend told me, "Sometimes God uses a negative situation for a positive one." This resulted in me taking a handicap driving evaluation (which I passed). This is a blessing because for 12 years, I told everyone my reflexes weren't fast enough to drive. *WRONG!* Additionally, this blessing would provide me with the opportunity to attend Sunday school, church, and weekly Bible Study.

Sixth, my barber-friend's mother was really sick and in the hospital one day. He talked to the chief doctor over the department at that particular hospital. However, the chief doctor had a severe speech imp...problem and my friend's first thought was "Hey, I don't want this doctor treating my mother." But then he remembered me, and that I have a speech problem but a sharp mind. The doctor was allowed to treat his mom. I considered this a God blessing.

Seventh, I moved to a Northwestern suburb of Detroit. I consider this move a blessing because of the new found independence I've experienced and the city's amenities which I will list. I'm able to grocery shop; go to the library, movies and to the malls, etc., on my own with no assistance. This is a significant blessing because for twelve years I didn't do any of these things or go to these places alone or hardly with anyone else. I always asked someone to please go for me. I would attend only a movie every now and then. This City subsidizes $8.50 of every cab fare (called, Senior Dial-a-Ride) within the City. A senior citizen (55 or older) van takes you to the mall once a week if you care to go, for $4.00, round trip. Also, for $4.00, round trip, the City's Senior Transportation van takes you to any suburb, for a doctor's appointment. That's any suburb, regardless of the distance.

Also, a County senior citizen connector bus will take you to most areas they service, with curb to curb service and with 48 hours notice. The cost for a round trip is a total of a whopping $2.00. Do you see why I've included these as blessings? I've never been so glad to be an over 55 year old senior citizen in my whole life.

MORE BLESSINGS

Eighth, I've had the same caregiver for over ten years. She is like a member of my family. My hat goes off to her because she has assisted me throughout and even before I realized (key word-realized) she was a blessing. I discovered what a blessing she was when she had to take off for three months a few years back, due to a death in her family. During that period I had to hire no less than three caregivers. One caregiver couldn't prepare JELLO-O! JELL-O, you all, JELL-O! I was so glad when my current caregiver returned I do believe I kissed her! Remember the "gooood" care nurse?

Ninth, a very recent blessing, I shared this past Christmas with my family. This situation which I observed was my (then) youngest granddaughter having photos taken with two of her three living Great Grandparents. How many of you have photos taken with your Great Grandparents? I know I don't. That's why it's a blessing to even witness.

Another blessing (*tenth*) and answer to a prayer. When my son told me, he had spoken to his grandfather, my 81 year father. My father told my son, *"I get down on my knees, every night and morning to say my prayers."* He also, told my son "Just like God gives, he can take it away." This statement by my father must have taken a profound effect on my son. Because, he said, "Every since that day in January, I have gotten down on my knees, every night to say my prayers." My son further stated, "The beginning of this year has been unbelievably fantastic." I think we all really know why. Thus, this was an eleventh blessing for me and an answered prayer.

I hope I'm not boring you with all these blessings but I feel people need to be shown examples of real concrete blessings from God. Actually, a lot of blessings from God are sometimes taken for granted. Also, a lot of people become jealous and envious, when someone is being blessed by God. I think that's silly. Instead, I personally suggest, that these people seek a personal relationship with our Lord and Savior. Then there would be no need for envy or jealousy because they would also be receiving blessings as well.

I guess my *eleventh* blessing is and this may seem small and insignificant, but a blessing just the same. Think about, when Jesus turned water into wine in the Bible, John 2 (NKJV). Jesus, among other reasons, showed his power and glory; he also did the miracle because he didn't want the bridegroom *embarrassed* at his wedding reception. This blessing by Jesus could be considered small but a blessing just the same.

My *twelfth* blessing is having my six pet Parrot fish and one Miniature Catfish all alive, in a 20 gallon aquarium for going on four years. It's amazing how the word of God is revealed in our everyday lives. Have you noticed, I've been quoting scripture like a preacher man, believe me, when I tell you it wasn't always like that (remember the rocket to hell?). As the worldly folks say, "I don't roll like that (no more)."

MORE, MORE, BLESSINGS

I will only speak about two or three more blessings. My ***Thirteenth*** blessing is the song, *I almost gave up but...God blocked it*. This particular song must have been real popular that year because I constantly heard it.

It's a blessing because the song vividly depicts how I felt during those three years of dark, self-imposed exile. Please, don't get it twisted! I never thought of committing suicide. I was, however, heavily depressed. I think there's a distinct difference between the two. I almost gave up trying to get better, physically. There is a BIG, BIG difference! Hearing the song 12 years later, post-stroke, blessed me by putting those three dark years of self-imposed exile in perspective. I was so *consumed* with "The" stroke.

Again, speaking of gospel music, when my barber/elder friend would visit I would make sure gospel music would be playing on my radio/stereo. At his Christian barbershop, the only music played the entire time is spiritual gospel music. One day, I asked my friend, "How do you listen to gospel music all day?" Then I stated, "I couldn't do it." Guess who, started to listen to only gospel music all day long? Yes, Mr. ME!

CONTINUED BLESSINGS & A ROLE MODEL

My **fourteenth** blessing happened while my son and a close friend attended one of my volunteer public speaking presentations, a few years ago. Afterwards, they both told me I inspired them, especially, with my independence. I told them that I took my 14 year independence for granted. What I should have told them (I must have been slipping that day) is that I wasn't independent, but that God was helping me do everything all those years. I just didn't realize it.

My *fifteenth* and *sixteenth* blessings are as follows. I have a deacon cousin, who recently told me, as a teenager he looked up to me for guidance and as a role model. I never knew it until he recently shared it with me. See, you never know who's watching you. Also, in that same year, I received an e-mail from a kid I knew from the neighborhood when I was 15 or 16 years old. In the e-mail he wrote he had observed me in my police sergeant uniform, driving a patrol supervisor vehicle, during my middle career days. He further, e-mailed that he was impressed with me before, but seeing me in the uniform was it for him. Shortly afterwards he joined the Detroit Police Department, and is currently a ranking officer.

The *seventeenth* and last blessing mentioned, in the summer of that year (and this may not be a big deal for some of you) I saw a man, literally stop and smell three roses. How many of you have observed someone literally stop and smell the roses? It was a small act, but very, very profound to me.

Finally, I just want to point this out, in no way was I bragging or being boastful, by pointing out some of the blessings I've received. Please, read (I promise the last one) Philippians chapter 3, in which Paul gives his personal testimony as an example that one MUST put no confidence in his/her own achievements, but MUST rely entirely on Christ.

This is exactly what I've tried to do. When we offer praise and testimony about how God has blessed us and when we tell others about our joyful relationship with God, it may inspire them. The results could be the leading of people to their own relationship with God. May God alone receive all the glory!

AN ALMOST CONCLUSION

Now, for the two word statement, you've all been waiting for...IN CONCLUSION! My future plans are to live to do the works of God, to emulate Mr. Preacher Man. I also plan to expect the unexpected, meaning to receive more of God's good blessings, and Miracles in my life. I plan to accept God's Love, Joy, Peace, Longsuffering (Patience), Kindness, Goodness, Faithfulness, Gentleness, and Self-Control, in order to:

- To prepare myself to experience God's awesome power, as a renewal and strength for my life
- To heal the brokenhearted, through God
- To tell the gospel through God to the poor
- To recover the sight of those who are blind, through God (metaphorically) and to bring them sight into the glorious light of God
- To talk to people and tell them there is deliverance and salvation from any consuming challenge, illness or problem
- To tell people to be concerned about living correctly and the importance of going to heaven and having eternal life
- To spread the "light" and "good news" of Jesus to each and everyone I meet

FINALLY, JUST CONCERNED BUT "NOT" CONSUMED!

I hope and pray that all readers of this book now understand why I'm now *concerned but not consumed*. Presently, I'm concerned about making it into heaven and having eternal life. I'm concerned about being anointed by God. I'm concerned about how many souls I can covert to God. I'm *concerned* about God forgiving me and others through His gift of salvation and eternal life. I'm concerned about living in a peaceful world. I'm *concerned* about studying God's Word with interpretation and understanding. I'm *concerned* about obtaining more wisdom and discernment. I'm *concerned* about keeping all Ten Commandments. I'm *concerned* about obtaining ALL nine "Fruits of the Spirit," not just eight. I'm *concerned* about new brain stem cell research. I'm *concerned* that in the next 5-10 years doctors will be able to perform surgery on the brain and eliminate severe strokes. I'm *concerned* that doctors will be able to produce new brain cells in the brain, enabling me to walk normally without a walker or cane. I'm *concerned* about this same brain stem cell research to rid me of the speech problem.

As you can see my list of concerns is quite extensive. The concerns could go on and on; too many to list. You can almost say, I'm *consumed* with *concerns* (joke). However, seriously you can see, I've flipped the script; my concerns now definitely out number my *consumed* behavior. In *concern* versus *consumed* as it applies to our daily lives, challenges and our decisions; one should never get to the point that they're so overwhelmed (*consumed*) by a challenge or situation that they forget to be concerned about what's most important, living a life with God. Lastly, I am no longer consumed by "The" stroke challenge!

MY PASTOR'S FAVORITE BENEDICTION

I'm giving my pastor's favorite benediction as an ending to this book. Every time I hear it, I become very inspired and uplifted. I pray the same happens to all of you.

"Remember you're loved, you're blessed and you're forgiven, Amen (May it be so)." Thank you, ever so much!

About the Author

Ron Sanders is a 23 year decorated, retired veteran, Detroit Police Department Homicide Detective Sergeant. He retired two years short of his 25th anniversary, due to a duty-disability stroke. During his 23 year career as a Detroit Police Officer, he worked several sections within the Detroit Police Department. Those sections included, Uniformed Precinct Patrol, City-wide Plainclothes Enforcement, Special Detail, with the Michigan State Attorney General's Office and Wayne County Task Force, Detroit Police, Internal Affairs Section, Uniformed Patrol Supervision, and the Homicide Section. While in his police career, Ron experienced at least fifteen (15) near-death experiences. He calls them Miracles and shares them throughout this book.

Ron currently lives in a NW suburb of Detroit. He is married and has 3 adult children and 8 grandchildren. Although "The" stroke has left him with an intelligible speech problem and the use of a walker (for balance), there is no other paralysis. He is able to do his own grocery shopping, banking, and has completed the process of driver's *retraining*. Ron enjoys spending time with his new wife, supportive family and belonging to a fantastic church, with a very dynamic teaching pastor.

To order additional copies of *Concerned But Not Consumed*, or to find out more about Ronald Sanders please visit his website www.concernednotconsumed.com or you can write Ron at Sanders' CNC Enterprises, P. O. Box 70 Farmington, MI. 48332-0070.

Discounts are available directly from publisher for retail, ministry, organizations that support stroke recovery and awareness or fund raising.

Zoë Life Publishing
P.O. Box 871066
Canton, Michigan 48187
outreach@zoelifepub.com
www.zoelifepub.com